HINDUSTANI LYRICS

HINDUSTANI LYRICS

RENDERED FROM THE URDU

BY

INAYAT KHAN

AND

JESSIE DUNCAN WESTBROOK

Sufism is the Religious Philosophy of Love, Harmony and Beauty

MOTILAL BANARSIDASS PUBLISHERS
PRIVATE LIMITED • DELHI

First Indian Edition: 1996

ISBN: 81-208-1435-5 (Cloth)
ISBN: 81-208-1436-3 (Paper)

Also available at:

MOTILAL BANARSIDASS
41 U.A. Bungalow Road, Jawahar Nagar, Delhi 110 007
8, Mahalaxmi Chamber, Warden Road, Mumbai 400 026
120 Royapettah High Road, Mylapore, Madras 600 004
Sanas Plaza, Subhash Nagar, Pune 411 002
16 St. Mark's Road, Bangalore 560 001
8 Camac Street, Calcutta 700 017
Ashok Rajpath, Patna 800 004
Chowk, Varanasi 221 001

PRINTED IN INDIA

BY JAINENDRA PRAKASH JAIN AT SHRI JAINENDRA PRESS,
A-45 NARAINA, PHASE I, NEW DELHI 110 028
AND PUBLISHED BY NARENDRA PRAKASH JAIN FOR
MOTILAL BANARSIDASS PUBLISHERS PRIVATE LIMITED,
BUNGALOW ROAD, DELHI 110 007

CONTENTS

CONTENTS—*Continued.*

FOREWORD.

OF the many languages of India, Urdu (Hindustani) is the most widely known, especially in Upper India. Both as a written and a spoken language it has a reputation throughout Asia for elegance and expressiveness. Until the time of Muhammad Shah, Indian poetry was written in Persian. But that monarch, who mounted the throne of Delhi in 1719, greatly desired to make Urdu the vogue, and under his patronage and approval, Hatim, one of his ministers, and Wali of the Deccan, wrote Diwans in Urdu. This patronage of poets was continued by his successors, and exists indeed to the present day; and the cultivation of Urdu poetry has always been encouraged at the many Courts of India. Some of the Indian Rulers are themselves poets, and find their duty and pleasure in rewarding with gifts and pensions the literary men whose works they admire. The Court of Hyderabad has for long had a circle of poets: the late Nizam was himself eminent as a writer of verse. The Maharaja-Gaekwar of Baroda is a generous patron of literary men, and the present Rulers of lesser States such as Patiala, Nabha, Tonk, and Rampur, are deeply interested in the cultivation of poetry in their Dominions.

In the eighteenth and nineteenth centuries many towns in India had extensive and flourishing literary coteries, and it is from the poets of that period that this handful of verses is gathered. The Mushaira—a poetical concourse, wherein rival poets meet to try their skill in a tournament of verse—is still an institution in India. Delhi, Agra, Lucknow, Lahore, Cawnpore, Allahabad, Benares, Calcutta, and Hyderabad, have all been, and some still are, nests of singing birds. Of the extent of Urdu literature some idea may be gained from the fact that a History of it written about 1870 gives the names of some three thousand authors, and that Tazkiras or anthologies containing selections from many poets are very numerous.

The poetry is very varied and of great interest. It includes moral verses and counsels, sometimes in intermingled verse and prose; heroic poems telling the old tales of the loves of Khusru and Shirin, of Yusuf and Zuleika, of Majnun and Leila, and the romances of chivalry; elegies on the deaths of Hasan and Hussein, and of various monarchs; devotional poems in praise of Muhammad and the Imams; eulogies of the reigning Ruler or other patron or protector of the poor; satires upon men and institutions, sometimes upon Nature herself, specially upon such phenomena as heat, cold, inundations and pestilence; descriptive verse relating to the seasons and the months, the flowers and the trees. Above all there is a great wealth of love poetry, both secular and mystic, where, in impassioned ghazals or odes, the union of man with God is celebrated under various allegories, as the bee and the lotus, the nightingale and the rose, the moth and the flame.

Most of the poets represented in this book write as Sufis, or Muslim mystics, and scoff at the unenlightened orthodox. For them God is in all and through all, to be worshipped equally in the Kaaba and in the Temple of the Idols, or too great to be adored adequately through the ritual of any creed. He is symbolized as the beautiful and cruel Beloved, difficult to find, withdrawn behind the veil, inspiring and demanding all worship and devotion. The

Lover is the Madman, derided by the unsympathetic crowd, but happy in his ecstatic despair. He drinks the wine of love and is filled with a divine intoxication. For him this world is Maya—illusion, and the true life is that which is unmanifest. He finds no abiding place in this mortal caravan-serai, this shifting House of Mirrors; for his Soul is ever passing forward on the high Quest. Knowledge and skill are as dust, and self as nothing, compared with the Love that goads and urges him on.

As a language, Urdu has a most composite ancestry, and comprises elements derived from the original languages of India, from Sanskrit, the tongue of the Aryan invaders, from Persian, from Turkish, from Kurdish and other Tartar tongues, from Arabic, even from Egyptian and Abyssinian; and later from such very foreign sources as Portuguese, Dutch, French, and English. The political phases through which India has successively passed have left their record in this hybrid character of the language. The process of its evolution really began, long before the Christian era, when Sanskrit—the language of the Aryan conquerors—began to commingle with the languages of the peoples in Upper India, or Hindustan. From this union came the prakrits, or vernaculars. The one which at the time of the Buddha was current in Magadha—parts of the present British Behar and Orissa and the United Provinces of Agra and Oudh—was known as Magdhi, and the message delivered by the great Teacher was recorded in that vernacular. This spread rapidly with the growth of Buddhism, and became the court and official language of a large part of Upper India. The language which was developed in the north and north-west was called at first by the simple name Bhasha (Bhakha), which means the usual tongue, but later took the name of Hindi, and is written in the Sanskrit (Deva-nagari) character.

At the beginning of the eighth century the Muslims appeared as conquerors in India. Mahmoud of Ghuzni, about 1,000 A.D., won great victories, and from that time Bhasha began to be modified in the towns. Four centuries later Tamerlane of the Mogul race entered India and took Delhi, laying the foundation of the Empire definitely established by Babar in the beginning of the sixteenth century. Hindi became saturated with Persian, itself already laden with many Arab words introduced through conquest and religion. The market of the army was established round Delhi, and bore the Tartar name of Urdu, which means horde or army, and thus, camp. It was especially at Delhi, after its rebuilding by Shah Jehan and its growth into the metropolis and literary and commercial and military centre, that the hybrid tongue took definite shape; it was named Zaban-i-urdu (literally, the language of the army) or simply Urdu, and was written in the Persian character. Even in its infancy it manifested a wealth of poetic inspiration derived from its varied ancestry.

The poets from whose work the lyrics in this book have been selected were mostly writers of voluminous Diwans, and they occupied various and diverse stations in life. Some were Rulers, some soldiers, some darweshes (devotees), some men of letters only. The name given is in each case the takhallus (pen-name); each has some special significance, as Sauda, the folly of love, Momin, the believer, Zafar, the victorious; and frequently this name is introduced, by way of signature, into the closing stanza of a poem.

ABRU : born at Lucknow, lived at Delhi, was a darwesh of the Order of Kalenders, and wrote an Urdu Diwan much appreciated for the ingenious allegories in which it abounds.

AMIR : Amir Minai of Rampur, one of the best poets of the latest period : a great mystical poet : his Qasidahs for Muhammad are sung by devotees : Court poet of Rampur : travelled to Mecca and Medina, and, after the death of his patron, Nawab Kalbe Ali Khan, came to Hyderabad on hearing of the Nizam's fame and interest in poetry : rival of Dagh, by whose side he lies buried in Hyderabad.

ARZU : a poet of Gwalior, where he held an important Government post in the days of Shah Alam II. (r. 1759—1806). He wrote his poems mostly in Persian, and was the author of a Dictionary of Mystical words.

ASIF : pen-name of H.H. Mir Mahbub Ali Khan, Nizam of Hyderabad, who died in 1911 : pupil of the poet Dagh (q.v.) and was an esteemed poet, and patron of poets.

DAGH : a court poet of Rampur : went to Hyderabad and became the teacher of the Nizam in poetry (see Asif) : lived there in great honour as Poet Laureate, and was given the title of Fasih-ul-Mulk (the eloquence of the nation) : his poetry is described as natural and graceful in expression : his proficiency was so great that no poet could stand against him in the Mushaira : he was of extraordinary wit.

FIGHAN : of Delhi : was the foster-brother of the Emperor Ahmad Shah (r. 1748—1754) and was one of the principal officers at the Imperial Court : famous for his piquant and witty conversation, and greatly skilled in jeux de mots, at which he spent his days and nights.

GHALIB : came of a distinguished Turk family of Samarkand : wrote in Persian as well as in Urdu, and held the position of Poet Laureate at the Court of Bahadur Shah (r. 1837—1857) the last Mogul Emperor.

HALI : a modern poet : pupil of Ghalib : recently dead : greatly admired, chiefly by the Muslims, for his poems calling for Muslim and Indian renascence. He received from the British Government the title of Shams-ul-ulema.

HASAN : Mir Shulam Hasan, born at Delhi; passed his youth in Faizabad and then came to Lucknow to join the literary circle there: was as handsome in person as in mind, and his verse is still popular.

HATIM : one of the early poets : born about 1700, he lived till near the end of the century : a soldier by profession, but in his old age renounced the world and became a darwesh : his cell was near the gate of the Imperial Palace, and many persons resorted to him for counsel.

INSHA : born in Murshedabad, lived in Lucknow about the end of the 18th century : enjoyed the favour of Prince Suleiman Shikoh : wrote verse in Turkish, Arabic, Persian, but was most famous for his Urdu poems, which are elegant in style and conception.

JURAT : of Delhi, celebrated for his skill in music, astronomy and poetry : became blind when still young : was pensioned by the Nawab Muhabbat Khan and afterwards by Suleiman Shikoh : author of an enormous volume of Urdu poetry composed of ghazals and of love-poems in the modern taste. Wrote satires on the rain, the cold, small-pox, etc. Versed in Hindu as well as Muslim poetry.

MAZHAR : of Delhi : family originally from Bokhara : learned in jurisprudence as well as poetry : many favourite poets were his pupils : was a Sunni, made profession of spiritual poverty, and was even reputed to be able to work miracles : was killed by a fanatic because he disagreed with the Shiah mourning for the death of Hussein : died in 1780, aged nearly a hundred years.

MIR DARD : author of a famous Urdu diwan : skilled in the sacred music as sung at the assemblies of the Sufis : lived the life of a sage, the Padishah often coming to him for counsel, though he himself never sought the Emperor's Court.

MIR SOZ : of Bokhari ancestry, had to leave his country in time of peril in the dress of a fakir : came to Lucknow, where he became tutor to the Nawab Asaf-ud-Daula.

MIR TAQI : born at Agra, in his later days lived at Lucknow, under the protection of the Nawab of Oudh : wrote many kinds of verse, but excelled in the ghazal and the masnawi, and was the author of a biography of poets : wrote his own autobiography in Persian, and also Persian poetry.

MOMIN : of Delhi : author of six long masnawis : skilled in medicine, astronomy and astrology, and deeply read in poetry : at first lived a gay and reckless life, in his old age gave himself to prayer and fasting, and acquired great contemporary fame : his work is considered to be the most delicate flower of Urdu expression.

MUSHAFI : belonged to a distinguished family of Amroha : lived at first at Lucknow, then went to Delhi : there he held famous literary reunions, at which gathered many poets of whom he was the inspirer and teacher.

MUZTAR : born and educated at Lucknow : his ancestors occupied an honourable rank at Delhi : was a pupil of Mushafi.

NASIKH : of Calcutta : belonged to the latter half of the 19th century : Deputy Magistrate and Member of the Legislative Council of Bengal.

SAUDA : born at Delhi about 1720 : a soldier by profession : much esteemed in his lifetime, and was a favourite at Court : excelled in all kinds of poetry, chiefly the ghazal, the qasidah, and satire.

TAḤBAN : of Delhi : as famous for his beauty as for ḥis poetic talent : pupil of Hatim, and was a friend of Mazhar and Sauda : was descended from the Prophet on both father's and mother's side.

WALI : of the Deccan, the first to write an Urdu Diwan : is considered the Father of Urdu poetry : born at Aurungabad, wrote in the latter half of the 17th century. He held a just balance between Sunnis and Shiahs, and did not flatter any Ruler in his verses. He knew the literature and art of Europe and wrote many mystical and spiritual poems.

YAKRANG: one of the officers of the Emperor Muhammad Shah (r. 1719—48): lived in dignity and honour at Delhi.

ZAHIR: a well-known modern poet, lived at Rampur at the Court of Nawab Kalbe Ali Khan, afterwards at the Court of the Nawab of Tonk, and finally at Hyderabad, in the literary circle of the Nizam, by whom he was much appreciated and rewarded.

ZAUQ: a celebrated poet at the Court of Bahadur Shah (r. 1837—57): was his teacher in the arts of verse: compiler of an anthology of poems: is said to have written one hundred thousand verses: is still highly popular and much quoted.

ZAFAR: or Bahadur Shah, was the Padishah of Delhi, the last Mogul Emperor, and lived 1768—1862: son of Akbar II.: was over 60 years of age when he came to the throne: himself a poet and a good judge of music and painting, he gathered round him literary men and artists: of fine countenance and distinguished manners, and extremely loved and admired by his subjects: skilled in all kinds of poetry, and some of his ghazals continue to be popular: author of a voluminous Diwan, and a Commentary on the Gulistan of Saadi: a clever caligraphist, wrote with his own hand passages from the Koran for the ornamentation of the principal Mosque of Delhi. His son Dara was also a poet. At the Mutiny in 1857 he was taken prisoner and sent to Rangoon: there he continued to write verses, and died at an advanced age. His portrait, which forms the frontispiece to this book, is from a miniature kindly lent by the Indian Section of the Victoria and Albert Museum, South Kensington.

J.D.W.

Dulwich Village, London.

October, 1918.

I.

Thou tak'st no heed of me,
I am as naught to thee;
    Cruel Beloved, arise!
Lovely and languid thou,
Sleep still upon thy brow,
    Dreams in thine eyes.
From out thy garment flows
Fragrance of many a rose—
    Airs of delight
Caught in the moonlit hours
Lying among the flowers
    Through the long night.
Look on my face how pale!
Will naught my love avail?
    Naught my desire?
Hold it as gold that is
Cleansed of impurities
    Tried in the fire.
Pity my heart distrest,
Caught by that loveliest
    Tress of thine hair,
So that I fear the shade
Even by thine eyebrows made
    O'er eyes so fair.

ABRU.

II.

Thou, Sorrow, wilt keep and wilt cherish the memory of me
  Long after my death,
For thou dwelt at my heart, and my blood nourished thee,
  Thou wert warmed by my breath.

My heart has disgraced me by clamour and wailing for years
  And tossing in pain,
Mine eyes lost their honour by shedding these torrents of tears
  Like fast-falling rain.

O Wind of Disaster, destroy not the home of my heart
  With the blasts of thine ire,
For there I have kindled to burn in a chamber apart
  My Lamp of Desire.

AMIR.

III.

Had I control o'er her, the dear Tormentor,
    Then might I rest;
I cannot govern her, nor can I master
    The heart within my breast.

I cast myself upon the ground in anguish
    Wounded and sore,
Yet longed to have two hearts that she might pierce them,
    That I might suffer more.

Utterly from her heart hath she erased me,
    No marks remain,
So there shall be no grave from which my ashes
    May greet her steps again.

O cruel One, when once your glances smote me,
    Why turn your head?
It were more merciful to let their arrows
    Pierce me and strike me dead.

No tomb, Amir, could give my dust oblivion,
    No rest was there:
And when they told her I had died of sorrow,
    She did not know—nor care.

AMIR.

IV.

This Life is less than shadows; if thou yearn
    To know and find the God thou worshippest,
From all the varying shows of being turn
    To that true Life which is unmanifest.

Beware, O travellers, dangerous is Life's Way
    With lures that call, illusion that deceives,
For set to snare the voyagers that stray
    Are fortresses of robbers, lairs of thieves.

The seer's eyes look on the cup of wine
    And say—We need no more thy drunkenness;
An exaltation that is more divine,
    Another inspiration, we possess.

O praise not peacock youth; it flits away
    And leaves us but the ashes of regret,
A disappointed heart, a memory,
    An empty foolish pride that lingers yet.

Upon the path, Amir, we journey far,
    Weary the road where mankind wandereth;
O tell me, does it lead through Life's bazar,
    Or is it the dread gate and house of Death?

AMIR.

V.

Here can my heart no longer rest;
    It tells my happy destiny,
Towards Medina lies my quest,
    The Holy Prophet summons me.

I should not marvel if for flight
    Upon my shoulders wings should start,
My body is so gay and light
    With this new gladness in my heart.

My weary patience nears its end;
    Unresting heart, that yearns and loves,
Convey me far to meet my friend
    Within Medina's garden groves.

My spirit shall not faint nor tire,
    Although by many tender bands
My country holds me, I desire
    The journey through the desert sands.

By day and night forever now
    I burn in Love's hot furnace breath,
Although there gather on my brow
    The cold and heavy sweats of death.

And ever in my home in Hind
    At dawn's first light, at evenfall,
I hear upon the desert wind
    The Prophet of Arabia call.

AMIR.

VI.

The light is in mine eyes,
Within my heart I feel Thy joy arise,
From gate to inmost shrine
This palace of my soul is utterly Thine.

O longing seeking eyes,
He comes to you in many a varied guise,
If Him you cannot find
The shame be yours, O eyes that are so blind.

I as His mirror glow
Bearing His image in my heart, and know
That glowing clear in His
The image of my heart reflected is.

O drink the Wine of Love,
And in the Assembly of Enlightened move,
Let not the darkness dim
Fall like a curtain 'twixt thy soul and Him.

Who gives away his soul
Forgets his petty self and wins the whole,
Losing himself outright
He finds himself in the Eternal Light.

Crazy art thou, Amir,
To wait before His gate in hope and fear;
For never in thy pain
Shall He yield up thy ravished heart again.

AMIR.

VII.

How can I dare profess
I am the lover whom Thou dost prefer!
Thou art the essence of all loveliness,
And I Thy very humblest worshipper.

Upon the Judgment Day
So sweet Thy mercy shall to sinners prove,
That envying them even the Saints shall say—
Would we were sinners thus to know Thy love!

When in the quest for Thee
The heart shall seek among the pious throng,
Thy voice shall call—If Thou desirest me
Among the sinners I have dwelt for long.

At the great Reckoning
Mighty the wicked who before Thy throne
Shall come for judgment; little can I bring,
No store of good nor evil deeds I own.

Among the thorns am I
A thorn, among the roses am a rose,
Friend among friends in love and amity,
Foe among foes.

AMIR.

VIII.

I shall not try to flee the sword of Death,
    Nor fearing it a watchful vigil keep,
It will be nothing but a sigh, a breath,
    A turning on the other side to sleep.

Through all the close entanglements of earth
    My spirit shaking off its bonds shall fare
And pass, and rise in new unfettered birth,
    Escaping from this labyrinth of care.

Within the mortal caravan-serai
    No rest and no abiding place I know,
I linger here for but a fleeting day,
    And at the morrow's summoning I go.

What are these bonds that try to shackle me?
    Through all their intricate chains my way I find,
I travel like a wandering melody
    That floats untamed, untaken, on the wind.

From an unsympathetic world I flee
    To you, your love and fellowship I crave,
O Singers dead, Sauḏa and Mushafi,
    I lay my song as tribute on your grave.

AMIR

IX.

Of no use is my pain to her nor me:
For what disease is love the remedy?
My heart that may not to her love attain
Is humble, and would even crave disdain.
O traitrous heart that my destruction sought
And me to ruin and disaster brought!
As, when the chain of life is snapt in twain,
Never shall it be linked, so ne'er again
My utterly broken heart shall be made whole.
I cannot tear the Loved One from my soul,
Nor can I leave my heart that clings to her.
O Asif, am I not Love's minister!
Who has such courage in Love's ways to dare!
What heart like mine such bitterness can bear!

ASIF.

X.

The eyes of the narcissus win new light
From gleams that in Thy rapturous eyes they trace,
The flame is but a moth with fluttering flight
Drawn by the lovelier lustre of Thy face.

This shifting House of Mirrors where we dwell
Under Thy charm a fairy palace seems :
Who hath not fallen tangled in Thy spell
Beguiled by visions, wandering in dreams !

The hearts of all Thy captive lovers stray
Hither and thither driven by whims of Thine,
Sometimes within the Kaaba courts to pray,
Sometimes to worship at the Idols' Shrine.

O Asif, thou hast known such grief and shame,
Shrinking beneath the cruel scourge of Love,
That all the earth will hail thee with acclaim
As most courageous of the sons thereof.

ASIF.

XI.

When shall the mocking world withhold its blame,
    When shall men cease to darken thus my name,
        Calling the love which is my pride, my shame!

O Judge, let me my condemnation see;
    Whose names are written on my death decree?—
        The names of all who have been friends to me.

What hope to reach the Well-Belovéd's door,
    The dear lost dwelling that I knew of yore;
        I stumbled once; I can return no more.

The joy of love no heart can feel alone,
    The fire of love at first unseen, unknown,
        In flames of love from either side is blown.

O Asif, tread thy pathway carefully
    Across this difficult world; for, canst thou see,
        A further journey is awaiting thee.

ASIF.

XII.

I ask that God in justice punish me
With death, if my love waver or grow less;
    Faithful am I indeed—
How can you comprehend such faithfulness?

To you alone I offer up my heart,
To any other what have I to give?
    No light demand I make,
What answer will you grant that I may live?

If on the last dread Day of Reckoning
I think of you, and in my heart there shine
    The beauty of your face,
God's Beatific Vision shall be mine.

Once I had friends, now none are left to me;
I see none else but you, because my heart
    Has wholly fled to you,
And thus I walk the ways of Earth apart.

I, Asif, am the chief of sinners held,
This dark dishonour will I not deny,
    But glory in my shame;
Where is another sinner such as I?

ASIF.

XIII.

O changing Wheel of Fate, still let there last
Before our eager eyes, still let there burn,
This vision of the world; when we have passed
 There shall be no return.

I thought that, leaving thee, rest would be mine,
My lost tranquillity I might regain,
But separation brings no anodyne,
 And kills me with its pain.

How can I traffic in Love's busy mart?
Thou hast won from me more than stores of gold;
That I may bargain, give me back the heart
 Thy cruel fingers hold.

O heart desirous, in Love's perilous way
Thy journey take and in his paths abide,
And thou mayst find perchance, lest thou should stray,
 Awaiting thee, a guide.

DAGH.

XIV.

O Weaver of Excuses, what to thee
Are all the promises that thou hast made,
The truth derided, and the faith betrayed,
And all thy perfidy?

Sometimes thou sayest—Come at eventide:
And when the evening falls, thou sayest—Dawn
Was when I called thee. Even when night is gone
I wait unsatisfied.

When in thy haughty ear they did commend
Me as the faithfullest of all thy train,
Thou saidst—I hold such lovers in disdain,
I scoff at such a friend.

O Mischief-maker, passing on thy way
So lovely is thy mien, all creatures must
Cry out—It is debarred to things of dust
To walk so winningly.

Why shouldst thou keep from tyranny anew?
Why shouldst thou not betray another one?
What matter if he die? Thou hast but done
What thou wast born to do.

Who cares not for his heart nor for his creed
Is the idolater. His worthless name
Is Dagh. O Fair Ones, look upon his shame!
He is disgraced indeed.

DAGH.

XV.

Thy love permits not my complaint to rise,
It reaches to my lips, and then it dies.
Now, helpless heart, I cannot aid thee more,
And thus for thee God's pity must implore.

Seest thou not how much disgrace and pain
The scornful world has heaped upon us twain,
On thee for beauty and the sins thereof,
On me for this infirmity of love.

Oft-times she will not speak to me at all,
Or if she deign to speak, the words that fall
Cold from her haughty lips are words of blame :—
—I know thee not—I have not heard thy name!

Deep in my memory was graved the trace
Of all I suffered since I saw thy face;
But now, Belovéd, thou hast come to me,
I have erased the record utterly.

With empty hands all mortal men are whirled
Through Death's grim gate into the other world :
This is my pride that it is granted me
To carry with me my desire for thee.

They say when I complain of all I bore
—It is thy kismet, what would'st thou have more?
My rivals also bear thy tyranny,
Saying—It is her custom and must be!

DAGH.

XVI.

I met you and the pain of separation was forgot,
And all I should have kept in mind my heart remembered not.

What cruelty and scorn I in your bitter letters knew!
No love was there; O Gracious One, have you forgotten too?

Strange is the journey that my soul by wanton Love was led,
Two steps were straight and clear, and four forgotten were instead.

There was some blundering o'er my fate at the Great Reckoning;
You have forgot, O Keeper of the Record, many a thing.

You took my heart, but left my life behind: O see you not
What thing you have remembered, and what thing you have forgot?

To meet Annihilation's sword is the most happy lot
That man can gain, for all the joys of earth has he forgot.

A Muslim on the path of Love beside a Kafir trod,
And one forgot the Kaaba, one the Temple of his God.

DAGH.

XVII.

What happiness is to the lover left
    Of peace bereft,
What freedom for his captive heart remains
    Held in her chains?

Sometimes unto the mountain peaks he goes
    Driven by his woes,
Sometimes within the barren wilderness
    Hides his distress.

Curses on Love, and may his home disgraced
    Be laid in waste!
To me the world and all the joys I sought
    Are less than naught.

Gladly, O Executioner, to Death
    I yield my breath;
And only wonder who shall after me
    Thy victim be!

FIGHAN.

XVIII.

If you should meet the Loved One as you stray,
O give my letter secretly to her,
    Then haste away
And do not tell my name, O Messenger.

O Morning Winds that from the garden blow,
Should you meet one like me forlorn and sad,
    On him bestow
The peace and solace I have never had.

O Eyes that weep and weep unsatisfied,
That shed such floods, yet never find relief,
    O stem your tide
Lest you should drown the world in seas of grief.

She need not have one anxious doubt of me,
She need not fear my further wanderings—
    How can I flee?
How can a bird escape, deprived of wings?

FIGHAN.

XIX.

How difficult is the thorny way of strife
That man hath stumbled in since time began,
And in the tangled business of this life
How difficult to play the part of man.

When She decrees there should exist no more
My humble cottage, through its broken walls,
And cruelly drifting in the open door,
The frozen rain of desolation falls.

O mad Desire, why dost thou flame and burn
And bear my soul further and further yet
To the Belovéd; then, why dost thou turn
To bitter disappointment and regret?

Such light there gleams from the Belovéd's face
That every eye becomes her worshipper,
And every mirror, looking on her grace,
Desires to be the frame enclosing her.

Unhappy lovers, slaves of cruel chance,
In this grim place of slaughter strange indeed
Your joy to see unveiled her haughty glance
That flashes like the scimitar of Ede.

When I had hardly drawn my latest breath,
Pardon she asked for killing me. Alas,
How soon repentance followed on my death,
How quick her unavailing sorrow was!

GHALIB.

XX.

I grant you will not utterly forget,
I hold you not unheeding and unjust,
    But ere you hear my prayer
I shall be dead and turned to senseless dust.

How little can one eager sigh attain
To touch thine icy heart to tenderness!
    Who can live long enough
To win the beauty of thy curling tress?

GHALIB.

XXI.

The high ambition of the drop of rain
Is to be merged in the unfettered sea;
My sorrow when it passed all bounds of pain,
Changing, became itself the remedy.

Behold how great is my humility!
Under your cruel yoke I suffered sore;
Now I no longer feel thy tyranny
I hunger for the pain that then I bore.

Why did the fragrance of the flowers outflow
If not to breathe with benediction sweet
Across her path? Why did the soft wind blow
If not to kiss the ground before her feet?

GHALIB.

XXII.

I had a thousand desires, for each of them I would have
 died,
 And what did I gain?
So many indeed are fulfilled, but how many beside
 Insatiate remain!

We have known of the tale of how Adam to exile was
 driven;
 More shameful in truth
Is my fate to be cast from the garden more favoured than
 Heaven
 Where she walks in her youth.

That living and dying in love are but one I have proved,
 This only know I
That I live by the sight of the beauty of her the Beloved
 For whom I would die.

GHALIB.

XXIII.

How long will she thus stand unveiled before me,
Shrinking and shy in maidenly distress,
How long, my dazzled eyes, can ye contemplate
    Her blinding loveliness!

No rest is for my heart by love tormented,
It cannot even win the peace of death;
How long shall it endure with resignation
    The pain it suffereth!

Like shifting shadows come the great and mighty,
And live their splendid day, and hurry past;
And who can tell how long the changing pageant
    Of fleeting life shall last!

O look on me, unhappy Asif, driven
As dust before the wind across the street;
How long has Love ordained that I should suffer
    Beneath the passing feet.

GHALIB.

XXIV.

THE WIDOW.

I call on Death, for Life is my distress,
And I myself a load of weariness
Weighing upon myself. Helpless am I;
Dared I to weep, then never would run dry
The fountains of my grief: I cannot speak:
Even the occupation that I seek
Goads me and wearies me. A jungle drear
This world and all its moving crowds appear,
And I the loneliest of all things on Earth,
Yea, lonely in the household of my birth.
Tired am I of my suffering through the years,
Even as mine eyes are wearied of their tears.
Spring comes again and brings the cooling breeze,
And Autumn with the rain among the trees,
Fair Summer with its moonlit nights of gold,
And Winter with its sweet and gentle cold;
These come and go, with morn and even-fall,
How can I tell how I have passed them all?
  Well, I have borne them all!

Hope gleamed awhile, but fled unsatisfied,
The flower sprang up. but drooped and fruitless died:
The silver bow of Ede shone above all,
But never came the looked-for Festival:
I saw the splendour of the season wane,
Never the benediction of the rain
Fell on my parchéd heart: the thunder loud
Pealed from the bosom of the darkened cloud,
But never came the long-desiréd rain:

I sought the fruit upon the tree in vain,
The thorn smote deep into my heart instead:
Across the desert wastes of sands I sped
Seeing the silver watercourses gleam,
But it was all a vision and a dream,
And thirsting in the desert I was left
 Lone and bereft.

HALI.

XXV.

Like silver torrents flow thy words to me,
But ah—I have no voice to answer thee.

My heart thy words have burnt with whips of fire,
Do they not burn thy lips, O Heart's Desire?

Thy promises are broken every day,
Yet—See my faithfulness!—I hear you say.

Candle-like wastes my body all these days
My flame-like tongue endures to sing thy praise.

O Hasan, I have spoke and sighed and sung,
Yet never from my heart my tale was wrung,
My secret grief can never find a tongue.

HASAN.

XXVI.

I cannot rise to follow her,
    Here in the dust is my abode,
For I am but her foot-print left
    Lying forgotten in the road.

Where are repose and patience gone?
    Where is my honour, held so fair?
All these are naught to me—I dwell
    In the black chambers of Despair!

INSHA.

XXVII.

How can I win that Hidden One
    Who sits within the secret place?
For even in my very dreams
    She wears the veil upon her face.

What heart is there in all the world
    Can bear thy cruel tyranny?
Keep then this broken heart of mine
    That thus thou mayst remember me!

JURAT.

XXVIII.

What kind of comforter art thou to me?
What help and solace in calamity?
No wound is there upon my bruiséd heart
But thou hast touched to make it sting and smart!

But yet, Beloved One, I ask in pain
When is the hour when thou wilt come again?
My soul cries out to thee in bitter need
—When wilt thou come—or wilt thou come indeed?

O Saki, do not pass my goblet by,
Although the feast is spread its lip is dry.
Be careful, O my tears, lest you should tell
The world my secret that you know too well.

O Sorrow, in thy tangled paths I go,
The Kaaba's gateway I no longer know,
But bend my head wherever I see rise
The arch that curves o'er the Belovéd's eyes.

MIR.

XXIX.

To whom shall I relate
The weary story of my sorrowful love?
O Friend, this is my fate,
This is the record of the pain thereof.

I prayed in vain to her;
She said—You weary me, I hear thy prayer,
It is thy messenger,
But when it pleads with me I do not care.

I said—Never again
Canst thou forget my faithfulness to thee;
She answered in disdain
—What mean thy love and faithfulness to me?

Life called to me
Telling me earth is full of hope and bliss,
Now undeceived I see
How foolish I to seek a world like this.

MIR SOZ.

XXX.

Even in the Kaaba courts my heart was moved,
Brooding upon the idol that I loved,
Mourning its loss. Now like a bird am I,
That painted in a picture cannot fly
Nor move nor sing; my heart is so outworn
With all the lingering sorrow I have borne.
Within my heart thy presence I have felt,
Within mine eyes, Belovéd, thou hast dwelt
For long long days. Who taught thee for a shrine
To choose a heart so desolate as mine?
Long time I told my friends my bitter grief,
And in the telling sought to find relief;
In silence now instead I take my rest,
And find that peace and loneliness are best.

MIR TAQI.

XXXI.

Wherever the Belovéd looks she stirs
    Trouble and longing sore and eager breath
And deep desire in all her worshippers,
    And some for her have drunk the cup of Death.

O Night of Separation, darkest night
    Of deepest grief, thy cruelty shall cease;
To-morrow I shall greet the dawning light
    Within the city of Eternal Peace.

O threatening Whirlwind rolling on thy way,
    I shall unloose thy knot, if thou but dare
With angry gusts to toss and disarray
    A single curl of the Belovéd's hair.

Sometimes her beauty goads and maddens me,
    I cannot bear her cruel loveliness,
But turn her mirror that she may not see;
    Why should I let her double my distress?

Heaken, O Momin, all thy life is done!
    In idol-worship at the Temple thou
Hast spent thy days, and thus thy years have run:
    How canst thou call thyself a Muslim now?

MOMIN.

XXXII.

I, like a wandering bubble,
  Am blown here and there
Shifting and changing and fashioned
  Of water and air.

Thou turnest thy face, O Belovéd,
  I cannot tell why,
Art thou shy of a mirror, Belovèd?
    Thy mirror am I!

When over her face she unloosened
  The dusk of her hair,
What need had the world of the cloud-wreaths,
  They fled in despair.

MUSHAFI.

XXXIII.

No man hath ever passed
Into the Country of Eternal Rest
With every longing stilled.
Who hath not lingering cast
Long looks behind, and in his eager breast
Held many a secret yearning unfulfilled?

Ah, Mushafi, to thee
Silence and thought in solitude are best,
For thou hast known
That laurel crowns are idle vanity;
There is no worldly rank thou covetest,
And what to thee is Suleiman's high throne?

MUSHAFI.

XXXIV.

Where has my childhood gone, where are its placid years?
For cruel youth hath brought passion and bitter tears.

To the Creator now I from the dust complain—
Beauty, the thing he made, brings with it only pain.

Long I desired and dreamed, waiting with eager breath,
But ere she came to me, Fate sent the sleep of Death.

To God as servitor I my devotion gave,
Now Love hath taken me, bound me to be his slave.

I, Muztar, die with grief, yearning unsatisfied,
Still hangs the purdah's fold I cannot draw aside,
Nor lift the needless veil woven of shame and pride.

MUZTAR.

XXXV.

The fire of love I for my idol know
    Within my bosom hides,
As in the mountain 'neath its crust of snow
    The flame abides.

Long have I yearned in vain to kiss her feet,
    I lay my weary head
Down in the dust, that thus my lips may greet
    Where she may tread.

No wealth have I, but like the moth I live:
    Since love demands a price,
I, like the moth, have but my life to give
    In sacrifice.

How has my bird-like soul been stricken low,
    Pierced to the very heart!
My love has used instead of bolt and bow
    A deadlier dart.

NASIKH.

XXXVI.

The wound upon my heart glows bright and clear
With such a steady and unwavering light
That in the darkness I shall have no fear
And need no lamp to guide my steps aright.

When of the darkness of the grave I hear,
The night of death, and all the pangs thereof,
I reck not, for one thing alone I fear—
The night of separation from my Love.

NASIKH.

XXXVII.

Shall I or shall I not console my heart
And win relief?
Or shall I sit in solitude apart
Nursing my grief?

O hear, while of my life now nearly done
Some sparks remain!
Soon I may be, who knows, O Cruel One,
Speechless with pain.

How can I to the fisher speak my thought?
Her snares are set,
My fish-like heart is by her lashes caught,
As in a net.

Look on my sorrowful mien, O Love, and tell
My hopelessness,
None of the manifold troubles that befell
Can I express.

Fair is the garden, Sauda, to thy view,
More fair appears
Her dwelling; let me all its ways bedew
With happy tears.

SAUDA.

XXXVIII.

I am no singer rapt in ecstasy,
Nor yet a sighing listener am I,
I am the nightingale that used to sing
In joy, but now am mute, remembering.

I know the drop within the ocean hides,
But know not in what place my soul abides:
I cannot read the hidden mystery—
Whence came I, whither go I, what am I.

My friends have paid due reverence at my grave,
And held my dust as sacred, for I gave
My humble life to the Belovéd's sword,
Killed by her beauty, martyred by her word.

I deemed life was tranquillity and rest,
I find it but a never-ending quest;
And I, who sat in quietude and peace,
Toil on a journey that shall never cease.

SHAMSHAD.

XXXIX.

Repent not, for repentance is in vain,
    And what is done is done;
What shouldst thou reck of me and all my pain?
    For what is done is done.

They said to her—Behold him, he is dead!
    How did he lose his life, unhappy one?
—O bury him deep in the grave, she said,
    For what is done is done.

This is the pain of love that I have caught,
    And what is done is done;
A thousand remedies avail me naught,
    And what is done is done.

For love I gave the honour of my name,
    And Good and Evil are to me as one;
Let all the world chastise me with its blame,
    For what is done is done.

The dust of Taban we could find no more,
    But yet nor rest nor respite hath he won;
His breath, his soul, floats round thee as before,
    And—what is done is done.

TABAN.

XL.

O Lovely One, when to the ravished sight
  Thou wilt unveil that radiant face of thine,
Each atom of the worlds, catching thy light,
Reflecting thee, bright as a sun shall shine.

Walk not, my flower, within the garden close,
Lest thou should give the the bulbul new distress;
For at thy glance each blossom turns a rose
To lure him with her cruel loveliness.

Victorious One, thou hast unsheathed thy sword,
The scimitar of thy beauty gleams again,
 So over all thy lovers thou art Lord,
Holding dominion in the hearts of men.

Art thou serene and calm and unafraid
When thou considerest thy tyranny?
Think of the reckoning that shall be made
Between thy heart and mine at Judgment Day.

WALI.

XLI.

O ask not frigid Piety to dwell
    In the same house with Youth and warm Desire;
It were as idle as if one should tell
    Water to be a comrade of the Fire.

O say not only that the Loved One left
    My lonely heart, and fled byond recall;
But I of rest and patience am bereft,
    And losing Her I am deprived of all.

Take heed, O Hunter, though within thy net
    Thou hold this bird, my soul, with many bands,
I struggle sore, for Freedom lures me yet,
    And may escape from out thy cruel hands.

YAKRANG.

XLII.

Thou shouldst have given to me the robe and crown
    And made me king of kings,
Or dressed me in the tattered darwesh gown,
    Poorest of earthly things.

O that I were thy fool to do thy will,
    Simple and led by thee!
What meaning have my knowledge and my skill,
    They have no worth to me.

Lo, thou hast made me as the dust that flies
    Unheeded in the street,
O were I that which in her pathway lies,
    Trodden beneath her feet!

My heart is as it were to fringes shred,
    Such wounds it had to bear;
Would that it were the comb, to touch her head,
    To tend her perfumed hair!

Long have I known that it was thy design
    To burn my soul outright;
O may at least the happy fate be mine
    To be the Tavern light!

ZAFAR.

XLIII.

Mine eyes were shut
    And yet I saw the shining vision gleam;
Now that mine eyes are opened, know I not
    Was it a thought that held me—or a dream?

Long to myself I said—It will be well,
    When I can see her, I will tell my pain:
Now she is here, what is there left to tell?
    No griefs remain.

Faithless she is to me, and pitiless,
    Despotic and tyrannical she is,
I looked for love, I looked for tenderness,
    I leant on vain impossibilities.

I listened to thy voice that stole to me
    Across the curtain where thou satst apart,
Desire came like a restless ecstasy,
    A sorcery that fell upon my heart.

When I had burst my prison, and was free,
    I saw no fetters held me, and I found,
O Zafar, that these chains that shackle me
    Are ties of self wherewith my soul is bound.

Zafar.

XLIV.

I care not if no rest nor peace remain,
I have my cherished pain,
I have my rankling love that knows no end,
And need no other friend.
I yearned with all my heart to hold her fast,
She laughed, and fled, and passed!
Lakhs of enchantments, scores of spells I wove,
But useless was my love.
I would have given my life to make her stay,
She went away, away, she went away.
Though I effaced myself in deed and thought
And brought myself to naught,
The dark and sundering curtain hangs between
I cannot pierce the screen.
And still I know behind the veil she hides,
    And naught besides
In all this changing Universe abides!

ZAFAR.

XLV.

That I should find her after weary years,
And that mine eyes should keep from happy tears,—
    That is not possible, this is not possible.

If she should come after these many days,
And if my wondering eyes forget to gaze—
    That is not possible, this is not possible.

Sometimes I long to kiss my idol's face,
Sometimes to clasp her in my wild embrace—
    That is not possible, this is not possible.

How can I let her seek my rival's door,
How can I bear the friends I loved before—
    That is not possible, this is not possible.

O Zafar, does she bid me to return,
And dare I, for I tremble and I burn—
    That is not possible, this is not possible.

ZAFAR.

XLVI.

Whence did the yearning of the soul arise,
The longing to attain the Heavenly Sight?
    Before what mortal eyes
Was manifested the Eternal Light?

When the soul understands and wakes to find
Thou hast within the heart of man Thy throne,
    It sees how arrogant and blind
The self that but its mortal self hath known.

Thou and I also were the seer and seen,
When none beside existed. Thou and I
    Have Lover and Belovéd been
Before this era of mortality.

How strange the turns in Love's unending game,
For neither Lover nor Belovéd lit
    The ever-burning flame:
Whence was the spirit that enkindled it?

The road that leads where pious pilgrims bow
In Kaaba or in Temple, Thou hast laid;
    And first of all wert Thou
To tread the road that thou Thyself hadst made.

ZAHIR.

XLVII.

Thy beauty flashes like a sword
    Serene and keen and merciless;
But great as is thy cruelty,
    Even greater is thy loveliness.

It is the gift of God to thee
    This beauty rare and exquisite;
Why dost thou hide it thus from me,
    I shall not steal nor sully it.

And as thy beauty shines, in Heaven
    There climbs upon its path of fire
The star that lights my rival's way,
    And with it mounts his heart's desire.

Even in thy house is jealousy,
    Thy youth demands the lover's praise
Over thy beauty, which itself
    Is jealous of thy gracious ways.

I died with joy when winningly
  I heard the Well-Belovéd call—
Zahir, where is my beauty gone,
    Thou must have robbed me after all.

ZAHIR.

XLVIII.

O Tyrannous One, when from my heart was drawn
    The fatal arrow, like a scarlet flood
My life gushed forth; but yet the one word Hope
    Was written in my blood.

Why should the Cosmos turn its wheel of worlds
    If not to search for thee eternally?
Why should the tireless Sun arise each morn
    If not to look for thee?

Alas my fate! before you came to me
    Already had I felt the touch of Death,
Nor was I spared before thy worshipped feet
    To offer up my breath.

For long, throughout the world, I sought for thee,
    Through weary years and ages of unrest;
At last I found thee hidden in my arms
    Within my breast!

Zauq.

FRAGMENTS.

Each morn I see the Sun in majesty
Come back to shine thy rival as before,
But O what ages has it taken thee
To come to me—if thou wilt come—once more!

ARZU.

Through Love did I the joy of life attain,
And walking in the way that He hath led
I found the remedy to heal all pain;
Why therefore is my pain unremedied?

GHALIB.

O burnish well the mirror of thy heart
And make it fair,
If thou desire the image of thy Love
To shine reflected there.

HATIM.

No fault is thine, Beloved, I do not blame thee,
Nor do I blame my rivals for their part,
I know my trouble causeless, yet I hearken
To my unreasonable, doubting heart.

MAZHAR.

What thou hast done, never an enemy
Would practise on a bitterly-hated foe;
And yet, my friend,
I took thee for a friend, and did not know.

MAZHAR.

Mayhap my sorrowful heart
Did not deserve thou shouldst bestow on me
Thy priceless love, but neither did it merit
Thy cruel tyranny.

MAZHAR.

She lighly laughed—And so is Mazhar dead?
Alas, poor helpless one! I knew not I
What was his trouble.—Then again she said
—I did not think him ill enough to die.

MAZHAR.

If I behold her, I am mad,
And if I see her not, I die;
O Love, to tender hearts like mine
Thou art a great calamity.

MAZHAR.

I ask for Allah's pardon, if I dare
To weigh and criticise what He hath done;
But when He made thy beauty shining fair,
What need was there for Him to make the Sun?

MIR DARD.

In spring, O Bulbul, go not in thy grief
To seek the garden, wandering apart;
But wait—one day within thy very heart
It shall arise, in bud and bloom and leaf.

MIR SOZ.

Some friend of mine, may be,
After my lonely death may let her see
How foolish were her idle doubts of me;
But no! how can I think the rolling Wheel of Fate
Should turn to favour one so long unfortunate?

MIR TAQI.

I, like a poor fakir,
Wander from door to door,
Bearing my load of pain;
But thou, O Ever-Dear,
Thou comest never more
Unto my door again.

SAUDA.

O changing Wheel of Fate, what thing is there
Thou hast not in thy myriad cycles brought!
Wilt thou, indeed, I wonder in despair,
Bring me at last what I so long have sought?

SAUDA.

I longed that the Beloved might come to me,
Or Patience come and in my heart remain;
But neither came, and now at last I see
The only constant friend I have is Pain.

TABAN.

False is she, breaker of all promises,
The heart's unending malady is she;
All this and more she is,
And she herself the only remedy.

Only in visions can I come again
To the Belovéd, and a shade she seems;
My lips desire in vain
The touch of ghostly kisses,
The shadowy kisses that I know in dreams.

O kind imagination, thou hast given
Eyes to my heart, and though She veil her grace
Fold behind fold, they seek the hidden heaven,
They find the secret beauties of her face.

I did not weep until my heart was lost,
So strange the bartering of love appears,
I gave the shining jewel of my soul
To buy these pearls—my tears.

The eyes say in reproach, O wayward heart,
What road of ruin hast thou led us in!
The heart complains, O eyes,
Beguiled yourselves, ye lured me into sin.

APPENDIX I

THE AIMS OF THE SUFI MOVEMENT

The Movement is based upon the Sufi Message brought to the Western world by Hazrat Inayat Khan in 1910.

In his studies as an initiate in one of the ancient Sufi orders, Inayat Khan recognised the basic love and wisdom through which humanity may realize the purpose of life. He saw these two principles as enshrined in the ideals of all religions. He held that by honouring all, and respecting their differences, a basis for mutual understanding could be reached which would not be possible by seeking to convert one to the views of another.

In pursuance of his vision he came to the West, and taught in Europe and America until 1926 when, shortly before his passing, he returned to India. He called his teaching the Sufi Message and to propagate it he founded a body called the International Sufi Movement. In the constitution are enshrined the following Sufi Thoughts:

1. There is one God, the Eternal, the Only Being; none else exists save He.
2. There is one Master, the Guiding Spirit of all souls, who constantly leads his followers towards the light.

3. There is one Holy Book, the sacred manuscript of nature, the only scripture which can enlighten the reader.
4. There is one Religion, the unswerving progress in the right direction towards the ideal, which fulfils the life's purpose of every soul.
5. There is one Law, the Law of Reciprocity, which can be observed by a selfless conscience together with a sense of awakened justice.
6. There is one Brotherhood, the human brotherhood, which unites the children of earth indiscriminately in the fatherhood of God.
7. There is one Moral Principle, the love which springs forth from self-denial, and blooms in deeds of beneficence.
8. There is one Object of Praise, the beauty which uplifts the heart of its worshipper through all aspects from the seen to the unseen.
9. There is one Truth, the true knowledge of our being within and without which is the essence of all wisdom.
10. There is one Path, the annihilation of the false ego in the real, which raises the mortal to immortality and in which resides all perfection.

The Movement has the following Objects:

1. To realize and spread the knowledge of unity, the religion of love and wisdom, so that the bias of faiths

and beliefs may of itself fall away, the human heart may overflow with love, and all hatred caused by distinctions and differences may be rooted out.

2. To discover the light and power latent in man, the secret of all religion, the power of mysticism, and the essence of philosophy, without interfering with customs or belief.
3. To help to bring the world's two opposite poles, East and West, closer together by the interchange of thought and ideals, that the Universal Brotherhood may form of itself, and man may meet with man beyond the narrow national and racial boundaries.

Regarding the aims of the Movement, we quote as follows from the words of Inayat Khan:

"The purpose of the Sufi Movement is to work towards unity. Its main object is to bring humanity, divided as it is into so many different sections, closer together in the deeper understanding of life. It is a preparation for a world service, chiefly in three ways. One way is the philosophical understanding of life; another is bringing about brotherhood among races, nations, and creeds; and the third way is the meeting of the world's greatest need, which is the religion of the day. Its work is to bring to the world that natural religion which has always been the religion of humanity: to respect one another's belief, scripture, and teacher. The Sufi message is the echo of the same divine message which has always come and will always come to enlighten humanity. It is not a new religion; it is the same message which is being given to humanity. It is the continuation of the same ancient religion which has always existed and will always exist, a religion which belongs to all teachers and all the scriptures.

Sufism in itself is not a religion nor even a cult with a distinct or definite doctrine. No better explanation of Sufism can be given than by saying that any person who has a knowledge of both outer and inner life is a Sufi. Thus there has never at any period of the world's history been a founder of Sufism, yet Sufism has existed at all times.

The present-day Sufi Movement is a movement of members of different nations and races united together in the ideal of wisdom; they believe that wisdom does not belong to any particular religion or race, but to the human race as a whole. It is a divine property which mankind has inherited; and it is in this realization that the Sufis, in spite of belonging to different nationalities, races, beliefs, and faiths, still unite and work for humanity in the ideal of wisdom.

The Sufi message warns humanity to get to know life better and to achieve freedom in life; it warns man to accomplish what he considers good, just, and desirable; it warns him before every action to note its consequences by studying the situation, his own attitude, and the method he should adopt.

Sufism not only guides those who are religious, mystical, or visionary, but the Sufi message gives to the world the religion of the day; and that is to make one's life a religion, to turn one's occupation or profession into a religion, to make one's ideal a religious ideal. The object of Sufism is the uniting of life and religion, which so far seem to have been kept apart. When a man goes to church once a week, and devotes all the other days of the week to his business, how can he benefit by religion? Therefore the teaching of Sufism is to transform everyday life into a religion, so that every action may bear some spiritual fruit.

The method of world reform which various institutions have adopted today is not the method of the Sufi Movement. Sufis believe that if evil is contagious, goodness must be even more so. The depth of every soul is good; every soul is searching for good, and by the effort of individuals who wish to do good in the world much can be done, even more than a materialistic institution can achieve. No doubt for the general good there are political and commercial problems to be solved; but that must not debar individuals from progress, for it is the individual progress through the spiritual path which alone can bring about the desired condition in the world.

The Sufi message is not for a particular race, nation, or church. It is a call to unite in wisdom. The Sufi Movement is a group of people belonging to different religions, who have not left their religions but who have learned to understand them better, and their love is the love for God and humanity instead of for a particular section of it. The principal work that the Sufi Movement has to accomplish is to bring about a better understanding between East and West, and between the nations and races of his world. And the note that the Sufi message is striking at the present time is the note which sounds the divinity of the human soul. If there is any moral principle that the Sufi Movement brings, it is this; that the whole of humanity is like one body, and any organ of that body which is hurt or troubled can indirectly cause damage to the whole body. And as the health of the whole body depends upon the health of each part, so the health of the whole of humanity depends upon the health of every nation. Besides, to those who are awakening and feel that now is the moment to learn more of the deeper side of life, of truth, the Sufi Movement extends a helping hand without asking to what religion, sect, or dogma they belong. The knowledge of the Sufi is helpful to every person, not only in living his life rightly but in regard to his own religion. The Sufi Movement does not call a man away from his belief or church: it calls him to live it. In short, it is a movement intended by God to unite humanity in brotherhood and in wisdom."

From *The Sufi Message of Hazrat Inayat Khan,*
Volume IX

Those desiring particulars regarding the activities in all countries of the Sufi Movement founded by Hazrat Inayat Khan should apply to the International Headquarters of the Movement as follows:

(for activities in India)

Sufi Movement India,
Dargah Hzt. Inayat Khan
129, Basti Hzt. Nizamuddin
New Delhi-110 013

(for activities outside India)

General Secretariat
Sufi Movement,
Anna Paulownastraat 78
2518 BJ The Hague
Holland

GLOSSARY.

Bazar—market place.
Bulbul—nightingale.
Darwesh—devotee, dervish.
Diwan—collection of poems.
Ede—festival.
Fakir—an ascetic in Islam.
Ghazal—ode : form of verse written in couplets, all in one rhyme.
Hind, Hindustan—Upper India, north of the Vindhya Hills.
Islam—The religion of Muslims : lit. absolute surrender to Allah alone.
Kaaba—central sanctuary of Islam, at Mecca, holy city of Islam.
Kafir—unbeliever, one who is not a Muslim.
Kismet—fate.
Lakh—100,000 : myriad.
Masnawi—epic poem, written in rhymed couplets.
Mecca—, Medina— } sacred places of Islam, in Arabia : the birthplace and burial place of Muhammad.
Muhammad—the Prophet of Islam (A.D. 570—632).
Mushaira—poetical concourse (Foreword p. 1).
Muslim—or Musulman; lit. one surrendered to Allah alone.
Prophet—(see Muhammad).
Purdah—curtain.
Qasidah—elegy or eulogy.
Saki—the cup-bearer, wine-giver.
Sufi—see Foreword, p. 2.
Suleiman—Solomon, King of the Jews: in Muslim legend lord over angels and demons.
Takhallus—pen-name.
Urdu—see Foreword, p. 3.